The Shaman and Shaman Magic:
Neo Shamanism 101:
The Way of the Shaman

By Kristina Benson

The Shaman and Shaman Magic: Neo Shamanism 101: The Way of the Shaman

ISBN: 978-1-60332-036-8

Edited By: Brooke Winger

Printed in the United States of America

Table of Contents

Introduction

When you hear the word *"shamanism,"* you may envision a man wearing a feather headdress, buffalo hides, brandishing medicine wheels and dream-catchers. However, this modern perception of a shaman is not historically accurate.

The word shaman originated in Siberia to describe the practices of the Siberian Native Peoples. The shamans of Siberia interacted with deities and spirits through prayer, rituals, and offerings, as well as through direct contact with the spirits. They would enter a trance that some describe as "ecstatic", freeing their consciousness from their body to go experience the other world.

A shaman may journey into other metaphysical worlds to gather information from the spirits, perform healings, guide the spirits of the dead to resting places, gain spiritual favor and power, or any number of other reasons. Shamans, and their communities, do not see themselves as self-appointed, or as volunteers. They are called to their tasks by the spirits themselves, and are then trained and recognized by their Elders and the community.

Eventually, the term "shaman" came to be applied to all medicine men and women of indigenous cultures. Shamans can be found across the planet, but exactly what they do is a mystery to most people. They have been called by many names -- doctor, priest, artist, visionary, master of ecstasy. In the past they have been branded as sorcerers, witch doctors, charlatans, and voodoo priests. While there are certainly differences from tribe to tribe and culture to culture when it comes to medicine men, or medicine women, the core practices are generally referred to as "core-Shamanism" - a phrase coined by Michael Harner, and described at length in his books.

In this conceptualization of the practice of shamanism, the shaman and his community experience, participate in, and express a set of beliefs that form a collective worldview. This view dominates all psychological and physical experiences. In the minds of people who share these sets of beliefs there is not a barrier between the physical world and the spiritual one, or between the dream state and reality.

Shamanism is the practice of these core techniques, either for healing or to gain spiritual knowledge. Shamanism is sometimes studied with the cultural reference, and sometimes without. Despite the perspective used, however, the essential nature of the shamanic practice does not appear to change to outsiders over time. I say "outsider" because American Indians are not evangelical, and while most are willing to educate non-Indians about themselves and their beliefs, they do not tend to welcome outsiders with open arms into their spiritual rituals. There will be a section on this later in the book in which I quote the American Indian Movement in order to communicate their point of view.

Since any Western words for the role disappeared along with the practice, *"shaman"* was adopted into English from Russian sometime in the 18th century, and has come to refer to .any community-recognized spiritual role models and seekers of the ecstatic trance-journey, whatever their culture or religion may be. The term *"shamanism"* can refer to the set of beliefs that are the cultural setting for the shaman or to the typical practices and beliefs of these spiritual leaders and specialists.

In the 20th century, an American movement grew that is usually called "neo-shamanism." It is a spiritual movement that seeks to adapt the practices and world-views of the Shaman into modern urban America. Neo-shamanism focuses on spiritual and psychological healing, and is often lumped in with other practices such as meditation, Wicca, and general New Ageism.

In this vision of shamanism, the Shaman can loosely be described as someone who has routinely had a direct experience with energy, and has the ability to harness energy to get power. This person's ability to channel energy makes him able to help people heal.

Well-intentioned and valid as this vision of shamanism may be, it does not usually make any distinction between the different practices of each tribe or culture. It tends to view and describe Native culture as a monolith. The truth, however, is that most American Indian religious practices are not terribly similar to those of the Siberian Shaman, nor to each other. Although the teachings of these movements may be useful, or even valid, they are neither traditional nor typical of Indian beliefs, nor are they shamanic in the technical sense.

Neo-shamanism is a very heterogeneous practice, and has, in many circles, come to be a catchall term for indigenous religion, earth-based religions, spiritual healing, or beliefs in totems, animal guardians or nature spirits.

This book will attempt to discuss "core-Shamanism" and "neoshamanism", as well as American Indian perceptions of Shamanism.

Part I: Neo Shamanism

The sections that follow will detail the practices and beliefs of neo-Shamanists, and neo-Shamans.

Life, and time, is cyclical

Like the Wiccan concept of the Wheel of Life, Shamanists believe, and behave as if, time is nonlinear. In this conception, time also exists on several different planes simultaneously, and is one with nature, the seasons, and the earth. The view of life, human or animal, is similar: we are born, we live, and someday each of us will pass away and become part of the Earth to again be reborn.

Preservation of Wisdom

The Shaman looks ahead, and tries to teach ideas and ways of living that will keep his or her knowledge alive for generations in the future. He or she also wishes to provide ample resources for survival for future generations. Because they are trying to convey such a vast body of knowledge to the student, the Shaman will usually only be able to take one, two, or three students in his or her lifetime.

Responsibility

The Shaman seeks to take responsibility for his own self-improvement without compromising the needs of those around him, or those of Mother Earth.

Asceticism

The Shaman does not seek to accumulate material riches. He or she is content with spiritual fulfillment, and does not seek validation through money or other material means.

Generosity

The Shaman believes that each should have what he or she needs, while giving what he or she can, to the Earth, to others, and to the community.

Education

A Shaman never ever stops learning. He or she advises others to gather knowledge, store or transmit it, and use it for the good of the community.

Respect for Elders and Ancestors

The Shaman realizes that all of us are here because of our ancestors, and would not exist had they not existed first. The Shaman does not, however, use this as an excuse to disrespect those that are younger than him. He respects everyone, from the youngest to oldest living member in the community. All have a purpose and each should have a say.

Respect for All Living Things

The shaman does not see animals, plants, or even entire ecosystems as deserving of any less respect than his or her fellow human beings. The shaman understands that we are a part of a web of life, and we all depend on each other.

Positive Energy

The shaman seeks to be positive, and seeks the positive things in life that make him or her smile and feel joy. The spirit and the body need goodness, wholesomeness, love, and positive experiences to survive and live a long healthy life. The shaman strives to live a healthy life, honors him or herself, and respects him or herself. .

Connection

The Shaman must be connected to all there is, and trust in his ability to stay connected to the spiritual realm while experiencing earthly pleasures such as hearing, seeing, smelling, feeling, and tasting. The shaman trusts his intuition and his communication with the other side. He also seeks to master the sending and receiving of messages to and from the planes of existence.

Memory

The Shaman is the keeper of tradition, history, the knowledge of our ancestors, and will ultimately come to be a walking library of knowledge for learning, healing, and helping. The shaman knows that our continued survival depends on remembering.

The Spiritual Worlds

Core Philosophy–Shamanism has a very specific understanding of the realms of spirit. It is divided into three "worlds". The Upper World, the Middle World and the Lower World.

They are all populated by powerful beings to which one can turn for help, teaching, protection, healing, guidance, etc.

Typically the Lower Worlds are where you find power animals. While it is tempting to relate to the Lower World by identifying with the Abhramic concept of hell, this is absolutely not the case. The Lower Worlds are wonderful, beautiful worlds that happen to be located below.

There are an infinite number of Lower Worlds, Upper Worlds and Middle Worlds, and combined they form a sphere shape. Traveling deep enough into the lower world will bring you to the Upper World.

Typically the Middle Worlds are to be journeyed to for questions about every day living and every day challenges, such as whether or not to take a certain job, or where to find a lost item.

The Upper Worlds are where one would find teachers, masters, and guides.

Part II: Practices of the Neo-Shaman

What do Shamans do?

Shamans work with the spirit, the mind, the heart, and the soul. They heal illness of the spirit, and of the soul. They gain knowledge and insight from observing the forces of nature and gain knowledge from working with spirits of animals, and their ancestors.

For the shaman everything is alive and carries a consciousness. In order to communicate with the spirit or consciousness of these entities, the shaman will shift his or her own state of awareness. There are many paths to this final destination, such as meditation, drones, or psychoactive plants. This experience can be described as ecstasy, a flight of the soul, or travel to the astral plane. The shift of consciousness that the shaman makes allows the free part of his or her soul to leave the body. The soul will then go on a journey to retrieve healing power, communing with the spirit world to get the strength and information he needs to help you. During the soul flight, the shaman still remains physically present, and has retained his state of awareness of the physical body throughout.

The shaman will heal spiritual illness by correcting imbalances, helping the subject regain his or her power, and regaining misplaced energy. Negative energy can remain stuck in parts of the physical body, and infect the mental along with it. These energy blockages are commonly called "psychosomatic illnesses" or physical manifestations of stress. The shaman will re-empower the subject by removing bad energy, and helping the subject refocus and reharness the good energy that remains. This is called a shamanic extraction.

Shamans can also be involved with earth healing by connecting with the consciousness of land, water, and sky. The shaman can determine reasons for drought, correct illnesses infecting crops, work with the weather, or heal sick ecosystems.

Many South American shamans are responsible for discovering the healing property of certain plants, which later formed the basis for specific medicines we use in the western health system today.

The effectiveness of a shaman is generally measured by the results he or she is able to achieve. The ability to let go of one's ego is a central concept for the shaman. If he cannot let go of pride and self-interest, he probably will not be able to enlist or channel the spiritual power necessary for effective healing.

Compassion is also extremely important. If the shaman cannot entreat the spirits to feel compassion for his subject, it is doubtful that the subject will benefit from working with that particular shaman.

Most of the techniques of a shaman are particular to the individual or culture—techniques will vary, and the shaman will do whatever he personally finds effective to call forth the energy for healing.

Shamanic Extraction

Shamans work with the spirit or the soul and they work with energy. Shamanic extraction is the process by which the Shaman redirects misplaced energy. No energy is truly bad, but if energy is misplaced, it will bring illness.

Where Does Misplaced Energy Come From?

Shamans believe that your emotion takes the form of energy and can be stored throughout the body, and, if left unchecked, this can eventually lead to illness.

People who are angry, or resentful, but fail to voice their feelings, often find themselves bearers of misplaced energy. Misplaced energy also could refer to the energy left behind from an injury.

The Extraction: Finding and Removing the Misplaced Energy

The shaman will first enter a trance-like state of consciousness to diagnose and find where misplaced energy might be in the body. The shaman will perceive the energy in some way that will indicate to her or him that it need to be removed. It may appear to a shaman as a hole in the person's energy field, or even as a beast. The way each shaman perceives that there is misplaced energy varies, but there is always a signal of some kind which says 'this does not belong here.'

Once the shaman has located the energy that needs to be removed, he or she will then consult with their guardian spirits or power animals, even merging with them, in some cases. This increases the shaman's power and allows them to remove the energy. It also protects the shaman from taking the energy into her or his own body during the shamanic extraction. This increase of power allows the shaman to pull the energy out without being affected or overcome by it.

Depending on the shamanic practitioner and the nature of the displaced energy this can be a very quiet process, or it can involve an elaborate ceremony or ritual. The shamanic practitioner merged with a power animal may move similarly as his or her power animal, may make the sounds of her or his animal, or may remain quiet.

The shamanic practitioner will dispose of the removed energy by transmuting it into a more positive life enhancing energy, or they may place it in water and have the water neutralize it.

Once the extraction is performed, the shamanic practitioner will fill the void that is created by the vacated energy in the person's body. They may replace it with healing energy, perform a power animal retrieval, or perform soul retrieval. The shaman will not leave a void for other energy to fill.

Protecting Yourself

You do not have to be a "shaman" in order to protect yourself from negative or misplaced energy. Visualization is a very effective tool that nearly everyone can use. To protect yourself from outside energy you can imagine yourself surrounded by protection—perhaps you can envision a green or blue shield that only allows good energy in. This can surround you as you go about your daily life, making you feel confident that no bad energy will compromise you.

When you are feeling negative emotions it is important not to shove them down, or build walls around yourself. The emotions need to be expressed and allowed to leave your body. You can write a letter and then tear it up, tell someone how you feel, or simply go for a walk in the woods and scream to relieve stress.

There are also stones, metals, and crystals that absorb negative energy, and stones that transform and lighten energy. You can have the stone in your pocket, wear it as a pendant, or place it on your dashboard or desk. People who engage in this practice will clean their stones with water and then recharge them to make sure that their energy stays potent. If you feel that your stones need a more radical cleaning they can be buried outside, kept in full sunlight for a day, or in full moonlight for a night.

If you would like to remove some of your own intrusions, visualization can be helpful. As you drink water imagine it filling your body with good energy and neutralizing misplaced energy. Or, go swimming and visualize the water washing the bad energy away. Lie out in the sun and imagine it melting away your intrusions and filling you with the sky's energy. Just be sure to imagine something replacing that which is removed so you do not find yourself with an energy void.

Properties of Crystals, Stones, and Gems

AVENTURINE: A good luck stone, especially in financial matters. Stimulates creativity, intelligence and perception. A great healing stone, it clears negative energy and vibrations as well as restoring general well being.

AGATE: General protection and healing, increases courage, self-confidence, and energy and promotes longevity. Solid, grounding.

AMETHYST: Reduces negative emotions (anger, impatience, nightmares); improves psychic abilities and imagery.

BLOODSTONE: An intense healing stone. It revitalizes love, relationships and friendships. It brings purification, orderliness, prosperity, and instills wisdom, enhances creativity, and supports decision-making. Warrior stone for overcoming obstacles calm ones fears of a real or perceived enemy, Boosts strength and courage and attracts wealth, healing, charity.

CITRINE: Reduces anxiety, fear, and depression; improves problem solving, memory, willpower, and clarity.

CLEAR QUARTZ: Inner strength, amplifies the properties of other gemstones, strength. It is probably the most versatile multi-purpose healing stone. Easy to cleanse, program or amplify energy and healing with. Can both draw and send energy. Powerful clear ones for meditation, sending & receiving guidance. Stimulates natural crystals in body tissue and fluids to resonate at new healing frequency. Possibly the greatest of all healing stones. Acts as an amplifier for psychic energy and aids meditation and visualization.

CARNELIAN: Improves physical energy, confidence, assertiveness; stimulate appetite, emotions, sexuality.

FLUORITE: Assists the conscious mind and body in analyzing conditions and situations in a rational and non-emotional manner, it enables detachment of the mind from the emotions so that the thought process can utilize the intuitive in achieving a higher level of self-understanding. Mental clarity. Helps to tap creative resources and experience the inner self. Enhances spiritual energy work, focuses the will and balances the psyche. Enhances ability to concentrate.

GOLDSTONE: Uplifting, reduces tension and stomach problems.

HEMATITE: One of the most grounding of all stones. Condenses confusion into mental clarity, concentration, memory, practicality, helps study, bookkeeping, detail work, and sound sleep. Confidence, will power, boldness. Egyptians used it to calm hysteria and anxiety. Helps adjust to being physical. Enables the psychic practitioner to unfocus from the physical world so as to receive psychic information. Aids in developing the psychic mental mind, optimism, grounds ideas, anti-depression. Calms and soothes, eases stress. Great stone for grounding.

JADE: Emotional balance, humility, harmony, wealth, longevity, compassion.

JASPER: (Yellow, orange, brown, green) Jasper is known as the "supreme nurturer" It reminds us that we are not here on this physical plane just for ourselves but also here to bring joy and substance to others, assisting others in releasing the bonds of negative energy. It is the stone that protects against negativity and helps one to be grounded to the stabilizing energy of the earth. Use this stone for long periods of hospitalization and when your energy feels low.

JASPER: (red) Powerful stone used for divination practice, worn to protect the individual during out of body experiences and vision quests by providing a solid grounding. It helps with conflict and aggression. Promotes grace and perseverance.

LAPIS LAZULI: Reduces anxiety, restlessness, insomnia, and shyness.

MALACHITE: Reduces depression & anger. Stimulates vision & concentration.

MOONSTONE: Soothes stress, anxiety, Enhances intuitive sensitivity via feelings and less overwhelmed by personal feelings. Greater flexibility and flow of life. For emotional balance, gracefulness. Balance of Ying-Yang energy. Can open your heart to love. It is also helpful in psychic work. It opens the spirit to the feminine aspect.

MOSS AGATE: Promotes agreeability, persuasiveness and strength in all endeavors. Improves self-esteem. Moss agate was used by the Native Americans as a power stone for the art of "cloud-busting" to bring rain. It is also said to help one in the acquisition of riches.

MOTHER OF PEARL: Wealth

ONYX: Protection. This stone helps to change bad habits, it is also an excellent grounding stone. Absorbs and flattens emotional intensity. Used for self-protection and to keep away bothersome relationships. Helps to release old relationships and keep away general negativity.

RHODONITE: Promotes self-esteem, self-worth and self-confidence, self-affirmation and self-love. Fosters ability to remain calm in arguments and resolve disagreements in a loving way.

ROSE QUARTZ: Emotional balance, love, beauty, peacefulness, kindness & self-esteem.

SAPPHIRE QUARTZ: A good healing stone to expand self expression and creativity, plus refining communication skills to new levels.

SNOWFLAKE OBSIDIAN: For grounding the physical and for protection. Used as a scrying tool to help the psychic unfocus from the physical and venture inward to receive information. Legendary dispeller of negativity, protects against nightmares and emotional draining.

SOLADITE: Healing of emotions and physical body. Assures clear communication. Eliminates guilt and fears and brings about clear vision. Elicits deep thought and calms overreaction by enabling one to think clearly.

TIGERSEYE: For protection, divination and inquiry into past or future lives. Clarity, optimism, and creativity. Enhances psychic ability. Stimulates wealth and helps to maintain it.

TOPAZ: The most powerful, electromagnetic of yellow/solar plexus gems. A strong, steady, high level gem for mental clarity, focus, perceptively, high level concepts, confidence, personal power, stamina. Helps with mood swings, insomnia, worries, fears, depression, exhaustion, nervous system stress, stomach anxiety. Radiates warmth, sun/light energy, protection. Brings emotions and thinking into balance. One can focus their desires through this stone, visual images in the mind are transformed into universal messages. Enables communication from other realms in the universe. Promotes peace and calms emotions, as well as promoting forgiveness.

TURQUOISE: A master healing stone that promotes spontaneity in romance and stimulates the initiation of romantic love. It balances and aligns all charkas and subtle bodies and can bring all energies to a higher level. A highly spiritual stone, yet grounding, it brings soothing energy and peace of mind. It brings strength, wisdom, protection, and positive thinking. A good general healer for all illnesses and excellent conductor. This gentle, cool, soothing stone is a Native American classic. For open communication, creativity, serenity, spiritual bonding, and upliftment. It opens the heart for giving/receiving. It symbolizes our source (spirit/sky) and spiritual love for healing, and help. Turquoise is the ancient absorber of "negativity".

UNIKITE: Healing of the soul. Guide to transformation and higher self. Reconciliation. Promotes balance and emotional stability. Transforms negative emotions into positive ones. A grounding stone.

Crystals for Specific Results

READINESS FOR ACTION: Amethyst, Ametrine, Fire Opal, Chrysoprase, Rhodonite, Turquoise

NEW BEGINNINGS: Garnet

CHEERFULNESS: Amber, Fire Opal

CREATIVITY: Ametrine, Amber, Garnet, Labradorite, Tourmaline

UNFINISHED BUSINESS: Aquamarine, Carnelian

FULFILLMENT OF DESIRES: Amber, Malachite, Hematite, Fire Opal

DEVOTION: Kunzite, Tourmaline

SOLVING DIFFICULTIES: Carnelian, Garnet, Moss Agate, Smokey Quartz, Tiger Eye

CONNECTION WITH EARTH: Petrified Wood

ENTHUSIASM: Aventurine, Fire Opal, Garnet, Labradorite, Rhodochrosite

FERTILITY: Chrysoprase, Imperial Toopaz, Moonstone, Rhodonite, Rose Quartz

FORESIGHT: Aquamarine, Turquoise

FRIENDSHIP: Emerald, Lapis Lazuli, Malachite, Peridot, Rhodonite, Watermelon Tourmaline

GOAL SETTING: Labradorite, Lepidolite, Watermelon Tourmaline

INDUSTRIOUSNESS: Rhodochrosite

INTUITION: Amethyst, Amazonite, Ametrine, Petrified Wood, Kunzite, Labradorite, Moonstone, Turquoise

LOVE: Chrysoprase, Emerald, Moonstone, Rhodochrosite, Rose Quartz, Ruby, Watermelon Tourmaline

LUCK: Agate, Ametrine, Aventurine, Amber, Chrysoprase, Garnet, Malachite, Moonstone, Sunstone, Turquoise

INCREASE MOTIVATION: Amber, Chrysoprase

ORDER: Aquamarine, Fluorite, Sodalite

POSITIVE ATTITUDE TOWARDS LIFE: Malachite, Chrysoprase, Imperial Topaz, Rhodochrosite, Sunstone

PROTECTION: Agate, Lepidolite, Smokey Quartz, Serpentine, Tiger Eye, Turquoise, Black Tourmaline, Watermelon Tourmaline

SELF-CONFIDENCE: Calcite, Citrine, Fluorite, Garnet, Imperial Topaz, Sunstone

STAMINS: Aquamarine, Garnet, Red Jasper

LOGICAL THINKING: Agate, Chrysoprase, Citrine, Kunzite, Lepidolite, Black Tourmaline

Power Animals

Shamans believe that humans are not the only creatures who carry with them power and wisdom. Power animals are an essential component of shamanic practice. This is the term that refers to the helpful spirit of an animal which adds to the energy of the shaman and is essential for success in any venture undertaken by the shaman.

Shamans believe that everyone has power animals - animal spirits which reside with each individual and acts like a "guardian angel. It is possible to have more than one power animal, and it is believed that each increases power and acts like a protective layer against negative energy and negative vibrations. The spirit of the animal also lends you the wisdom of its kind. For example, a hawk spirit will give you hawk wisdom, and lend you some of the attributes of hawk.

Everyone is thought to have a few of these guardian power animals, and over the course of the average lifetime, several power animals. If a power animal leaves and one does not come to take its place the individual is considered vulnerable to illness and bad luck.

Any type of animal can be a power animal—they do not have to be mammals and can be reptiles, insects, or sea creatures. It is possible to have a domesticated animal, but it is more likely to have a wild untamed animal serve in the capacity of a power animal. Plants too have their place, but are considered spirits, and not guardians.

The power animal can serve many functions: a particular power animal can come to help you with an issue that is very specific for you, or can provide a constant, comforting presence.

Honoring the Power Animal

There are many ways to honor your power animal. Honoring your Power Animal can be very personal, and it is possible that he will ask you what to do. Other times, it will be up to you to show your appreciation for your animal.

Wear Clothing or Jewelry Decorated With Images of Your Animal.

You can also do this to constantly remind yourself of the powers that your animal gives you, and that he is always present for when you need him.

Research the Habits of Your Animal.

Animals are fascinating creatures, with so much to teach us. Find out where your animal lives. What kinds of noises does she make, and what do they mean? Is her behavior as you expected?

Visit the Habitat of Your Animal.

Visiting his home will help you connect with and understand him better than before.

Donate to Organizations that Protect Your Animal.

Is his habitat threatened? Is he endangered? What can you do to make sure that this animal continues to be a part of Earth's community. Are there groups dedicated to him? For instance, a Parrot Enthusiast group, or a Friends of the

Whale club near you? Find out how you can help your animal.

Visit Your Animal.

This can be done when you meditate, or you can physically go see your animal. Sometimes you can go outside your own house and see him, depending on where you live. Other times, you may have to go to a zoo, or a wildlife preserve

Finding Your Power Animal

Power Animals are usually a reflection of our deepest selves, our spirits, and our souls. They also represent qualities that we may not even be aware that we have. Your personal Power Animal may change depending upon your specific needs. If you are dispirited, your animal is far away from you and needs to be called back, or replaced with another, more willing Animal spirit.

All animals—even those thought of as vermin—have gifts to give, and are potentially positive spirits. Your Power Animal can talk to you, in words or in feelings, and will understand you. This animal is there to help you and, unlike a pet, doesn't need your care or guardianship.

In order to find your Power Animal, all you need is time, and patience.

Select a time where you can remain undisturbed. You will want to be somewhere quiet, and where you feel safe. If quiet is impossible to guarantee, you may use earplugs or noise canceling headphones, put on soothing, meditative music, or use a white noise machine.

Once you have found a suitable time, make a pleasant space for yourself. Make sure that the room—or area (you can be outside if you want)—is free from distractions. Make sure that it is clean, and smells either neutral, or pleasant.

Now, you're ready to open yourself to your Power Animal. Lie down on your back, feet together at the ankles, tops of feet relaxing to fall outwards. Arms are at your sides, fingers relaxed. Breathe through your nose at a pace that is natural. Scan your body for tension or stiffness, and relax. Even the eyes, cradled in the sockets, should be still and relaxed.

Visualize yourself walking down a path. It can be night or day. The path can be through a meadow, in the snow, or in the desert. Whatever feels right to you is fine. The path leads to the opening of a cave. In the cave is your power animal. Sit outside the cave and wait as long as it takes for your animal to reveal itself.

When you see it, you will know. Do not send back your Animal if you are disappointed—say, if it's Cockroach, or Chicken. Sending him back will anger him, and is a product of the ego. Whichever animal you see is the one for you. When you see the Animal, take some time to get to know him or her. Is it a him or a her? What color? Is she old, young? A parent? Will she let you touch her? Do you name the Animal, or does it already have a name?

When you are done getting to know your animal, or if he retreats back to the cave, remain in meditation for a while to reflect on what you just saw. When you are ready, open your eyes, breathe, and slowly sit up. Now you may look up your animal to see which properties he or she possesses, and how you can benefit.

It is certainly possible to have more than one Power Animal. In particularly trying times, it is also possible to actively call on animals for help. This will not offend your Power Animal, and he will still be yours even if another animal is coming to your aid.

During periods of difficulty or change, you may again want to go to your cave and see if your Power Animal is still there, or if a different animal emerges. Sometimes, your Power Animal will still be there. Others, a different Animal will have taken his place. This is your new Power Animal for the time being.

Calling on the Animal Spirit for Help

Sometimes, your Power Animal's particular set of strengths will not help you meet a challenge. It is possible to retain your Power Animal while calling on another for help. There are four different types of Animal Guides that can come to your aid in times of trouble.

Messenger Guide

This animal quickly comes into your life and stays only long enough for you to figure out the message, and how it affects you. The message itself can be spiritual in nature, it can be a call to action, or it can be a warning. Sometimes the Animal will appear when you call to it for help; other times it will be sent to you, and it will be up to you to interpret why it was sent. For instance, you may see a nature program about a Lion. Then you might go for a walk and see a billboard advertising something with a Lion. Later that evening, a friend may mention something about drinks at the Red Lion Inn. It is possible that Lion is trying to send you a message, and will depart once you figure out what that message is.

A Shadow Animal Guide

This animal is one that scares you, such as a Cockroach, a Snake, or a large Dog. Its purpose is to teach a lesson that you may not have learned because of excessive hubris, or greed. A Shadow Guide will not stop returning until it inspires a change of action or lifestyle. For instance, you may be living an extraordinarily unhealthy lifestyle, and continue seeing or hearing about vultures at every turn. Until you make a change, you will continue seeing Vulture.

A Journey Animal Guide

A journey animal guide appears when you are forced to make a decision as to which path to take. It can be a friendly traveling companion if the path is right, and remains at your side until the journey is complete. It can be a friendly traveling companion if the path is right; if the animal is not friendly, call to your Power Animal for guidance to see if you've made the right decision.

Your Power Animal

Your personal power animal remains a part of you throughout large periods of time in your life, or even your entire life, and reflects your inner-spiritual self. You may have more than one and new ones may come during an expected time. Its powers are always there for you and serve as a constant reminder of your inner powers and oneness with nature.

The Shamanic Trance

There are many paths to the Trance State, or State of Ecstasy. Some hints, then, for safe trance-working: preparation is vital. To engage in a trance-state properly you first and foremost need time alone, where there is a guarantee that you will not be interrupted for hours. It is important to have distance from the stresses of daily life, and it also helps to be free from physical illness or injury, lest you focus overly on the physical body. The specifics are up to you. You can do trance work at night or during the day. You may use incense, music, or rhythm.

Beginners may want to refrain from overeating or drinking too much before you start your work, lest you become distracted by the need for urgent and frequent visits to the toilet. Some techniques can be performed alone, but others require the grounding force of another person. The ultimate goal is to achieve a state that is much like meditation: one where the mind is free from the body, where all is still, and the passing of time is irrelevant and unnoticed. It can be described as a state complete certainty, clearness, and stillness.

Using the Rhythmic Body to Induce Trance States

Dancing and swaying are the two natural ways of expressing rhythm with the body. The trance walking and hyperventilation as two special kinds of trance working are belonging to this category, too.

Traditionally the Sufis use a whirling dance to induce a trance state. Some sects of Sufi shout Allah! Allah! While turning their heads sharply to the left and to the right with each syllable. Some cultures will shake in order to induce a state of trance. The frequency of the shaking can determine the trance-experience: slow swaying induces different states then fast shaking or shuddering.

Some also report that walking or running can quickly induce a state of euphoria, known as "runner's high". This may not be the type of trance one would associate with shamanism, but it is a trance nonetheless. Athletes who complete in ultra marathons—distances of a hundred miles or more—work themselves into a trance state as they rhythmically put one foot in front of the other, for hours, or even days.

Another method of inducing Trance is hyperventilation. This results in lowered amounts of CO_2 in your blood. The symptoms of it are tickling of the extremities, headache, claw-like hand-position and generalized cramps. During trance the ventilation patterns changes again, but is still keeping the state up for a time. It is a secure way of inducing trance but some find it uncomfortable and unpleasant to the point of distraction.

Rhythms

Often the trance-inducing power of the drum is being explained by the influence that certain beating, repetitive, constant sounds have on the brain-wave patterns of the listener. A rhythm of 4 to 5 bps is said to be ideal. Very often other instruments are used like rattles, sticks, bows, singing bowls, didgeridoos or the voice. Siberian shamans are understood to start playing their drums after they have reached the trance-state, not before. Nearly any rhythmic, pleasant, repetitive sound produced at a reasonable volume can be used to entrance the audience. You can play the drum yourself as you reach for this state, or you can play a recording. This is also an ideal way to use your time if at a drum circle.

Optical Induction of Trance

Watching constant and repeating patterns can induce trance just about as well as hearing them. A swinging pendulum, or kaleidoscope-like images, are examples of optical induction of trance that you may have seen.

Mind Focus as Trance Induction.

Some describe this practice as meditation; others as "gazing". Those who "gaze" focus their attention specifically on pictures, power objects, mirrors or mantras, and seek to block all other thoughts, perceptions, or cognitions from entering their minds.

Those who use pictures to induce a trance start by staring on the picture without any motion. They gaze on the picture without moving the eyeballs for as long as possible. After a few moments the eyes water a lot, but this should be ignored. In fact, the staring should become more focused with eyes wider. Eventually, your vision will cloud, and you will be in a trance state.

Others find pictures too distracting, and use objects such as mirrors, crystal balls, or crystals. A black mirror can be used as a gate or window into the spirit world. Gazing on crystals, stones or power objects unlocks the hidden spirits and energies of these items.

Mantras

A mantra is a phrase that is repeated over and over, in a chant, such as "om". If using this method of trance induction, repeat the mantra in your mind until there is nothing else, no other thoughts. Then let your mind unfold.

With this technique, as with all others, patience is a virtue. Trance is not necessarily induced in five minutes, or on the first five attempts.

Inducing Trance Through Body Postures

Probably the best example of this is yoga, which brings us to the next section...

Yoga and Shamanism

Aleister Crowley combined within his work the teachings of eastern systems with western magic, advocating for control of the body as well as control of the mind. Crowley adapted the Asana (poses) and the Pranayama (breathing) of the Indian yogic system as a means to these ends.

Some practitioners of neo-shamanism readily incorporate yoga into their practice. Others incorporate it into their lifestyles, but feel that it is separate from shamanism because it stifles creativity and spontaneity. Still others argue that shamanism came from yoga, and vice versa. Since there is no one way to practice shamanism, or, really, yoga, you may incorporate yoga into your work or not, as is your preference.

The Animal Dance

In the legends and myths of all cultures you can find hints about humans that perform dances and engage in rituals in order to honor animals, and to spiritually cross over into the animal world. Some even believe that these dances give the animal the opportunity to take over, or partially embody, the shaman. The animal "rides" the body of the shaman and takes over the active part, ousting the ego of the shaman from its conducting position to the role of a watcher. During the animal dance the animal heals the shaman, or the shaman can do an ecstatic flight of the soul.

Conducting and engaging in the animal dance requires time for preparation, as well as time for relaxing and grounding afterwards. There are many ways to enter the state of ecstasy during the animal dance: drugs, drums, breathing, certain sacrifices, imagination and imitation are all paths to this destination. The animal dance can continue for as long as you wish. When it's over, take time to come back from this intense experience, and lay down on the ground in order to center yourself.

Costumes and Animal Dances

Shamans often use costumes and masks that depict or represent their animal guides. Costumes may serve different functions, and it is necessary to ask the spirits about details of making, using and caring for their mask or their costume. Dancing costumes are extremely powerful tools of the art, and need to not be made of animal parts, except those that the spirits offers to you. Materials like iron, wood, felt and synthetic materials are fine for manufacturing a costume. Attach little bells to the costume to drive away unwanted spirits and intensify the trance.

Soul Retrieval

Neoshamanistic literature often writes about the phenomenon of soul loss, or soul fragmentation, at great length. There are many different descriptions of the anatomy of the soul, but what they usually have in common is the visualization of the soul as an entity that has more than one part. In the neo-shamanist vision of the soul, most of it is inside of one's immediate sphere of influence.

Accidents, operations, trauma, psychic pressure or stress can cause damage to, or even fracture of, the soul. During these situation the soul decides to save the part exposed to the threat by splitting it and hiding it somewhere in the spirit world. Most of the time the part of the soul returns after a time, but until then, the subject experiences soul loss, or a fractured soul.

Symptoms like listlessness, sleeplessness, emotional emptiness, depression, or catatonia can occur. Once recognized as soul loss the shamanic practitioner can ask his power animal or other spirits to guide him to the lost parts of the client's soul. Then the shaman persuades the soul parts to return to the subject, brings them back, and literally blows them into the crown chakra.

It is absolutely necessary to seal the chakra after blowing in the soul parts, and the subject must welcome his once lost soul parts back. Furthermore, Soul Retrieval can be very emotional, and many will need comfort after they go through this intense experience. Sometimes it helps the subject to have a trusted friend, family member, or pet in the room.

In other situations, there is a part of the soul that has become infected, or damaged. In this case, the shaman will run his hands over the aura of the subject, and will usually find the infection in this manner. Once he has located it, he will literally suck out the infection, being careful not to swallow it himself, and then guide the client through meditation and visualization so he or she can recover.

Divination

Many associate divination with Tarot or astrology, and
regard these practices as the as the primary methods of
achieving the unknowable. Shamans, however, engage in a
form of divination when they ask the spirits or the forces of
nature for advice and knowledge. To divine something is to
receive insight on topics in the future, present or past.

There are some uniquely "neo-shamanist" methods of
receiving and making an oracle or prophecy. The simplest
way is to have a question, take your rattle, drum, or drone
with you and take a walk. Then, ask your spirits and
animals to show you a place where you can get the answer.
When you reach this place, close your eyes and begin to
rattle or drum until the spirits tell you to stop. Immediately
after you stop rattling - within 3 seconds - the first
impression you are receiving is the answer. After you
received the reply to your question it may be necessary to
understand the answer. You can make a shamanic journey
or meditate on the results for deeper understanding.

Another way is the oracle of stones. Look at the stone in
order to find structures on its surface which resemble
landscapes, animals, faces or persons or everything you

can imagine. These images are talking to you and telling you the answer to your question. Return the stone to its place where it belongs (if it was small enough for you to pick up and examine) and thank the spirits for their help. A really interesting and beautiful way to answer questions and receive prophecies is to go on a vision quest, or a retreat.

The Power of Singing

The Power Song is regarded as a very powerful tool in the neo-Shamanic quest.

If you have a good connection with your spirits they will provide you with instructions, such as "howl like a coyote" or "sing like the wind in the trees". Perhaps you learn a melody from your shamanic teachers or they tell you to, sing however you want. The songs you learn in this way are your power songs. Strange and unusual melodies or even animal sounds are within the reaches of a power song as well as most beautiful tunes.

If this doesn't suit you, there are other paths to finding your spirit song. Take for yourself a little time at the evening. Experiment with your voice and see what sounds come out. Free yourself from the burden of judgment—just enjoy what you are doing, and the act of freely singing without worrying about what comes out. At the first signs of stress or fatigue, however, stop and allow your voice to rest. Some day you will find sounds or tunes fitting to your intuition and your being.

Power songs are extremely individualistic and cannot be copied by other practitioners, although you can sing the songs of others to feel their unique powers and understand the experience of that individual.. Power songs can change over time, reflecting the development and personality of its owner, and it's not uncommon to have more than one power song. Of course your own power song has some trance inducing effects. To enter a trance, you can always begin by singing your power song.

Offerings

Sometimes in the course of your shamanic practice, the spirits may demand an offering. It is important to keep in mind that these offerings have to be in relation to the deeds done by your spiritual guides. They can range from simple prayers and small sacrifices to more complex things like rituals or quests. Spirits are easy to satisfy, usually. Fresh fruits or vegetables, tobacco offerings, honey or milk, small coins, incense sticks should be sufficient.

If your spirits start to demand animal sacrifices you should be very rigorous with the interpretation. Most of the time these demands are symbolic, however. Animal sacrifices are not for beginning shamans and are nothing to take lightly. Sacrificing animals can lead to profound guilt, or conversely, awaken inborn powers that you never knew existed.

The Shamanic Toolbox

The most common items decorating the homes of neo-Shamanists include rock-crystals, semi-precious stones, gems, medicine wheels, drums, and tarot decks. You will doubtlessly also find dream catchers, feathers, furs, drums and rattles etc. Many people buy spiritual and pseudo-spiritual items and artifacts and collect them at their homes. Sometimes they feel that it sets an atmosphere conducive to their Shamanistic work; other times, they merely have the urge to collect things.

The longer you dabble in neo-shamanism the more opportunities you will have to get some instructions by the spirits as to the kind of item which you have to create, invent, buy or find in the nature. Any item the shaman uses for his spiritual work can be considered as "holy" These items you make, buy, or receive during your shamanist-career are generally considered to help you in your shamanic practices.

Developing your own abilities without any crutches is highly recommended, but sometimes people really benefit from having a physical object to focus on. It is important, however to develop a kind of compromise between the path of the empty hand, and the syndrome of "Dumbo's Magic Feather" As soon as you can *only* work *with* these things, you are depending on them - and that is to be avoided.

If you do choose to use physical objects in your work, it is important to keep them away from the hands of others to avoid energetic pollution. A trusted teacher or friend can handle an item, if you want his or her energy, but if others handle it, it must be spiritually recharged. it.

Within your shamanic practice you may receive gifts from nature and the spirits. These gifts should always be treated with respect. The feather, the fur, the stone or whatever else you are given by the spirits has already been charged, and it is always necessary to ask the inhabiting spirit why it is appearing in your life. The same can apply to the drum, the rattle, or your whole shamanic costume, but is especially true with animal parts, such as claws and furs. You have to get in contact with the spirit of this animal, because a living being had to die for the object to be given to you.

It is, of course, possible to purchase all manner of shamanic tools in New Age stores. It is often impossible to tell how the store got the items—for instance, was the drum made in a sweatshop in Thailand? Were the crystals mined using slave labor? Etc. If an object from such a store calls to you, and you cannot find another way, try to make sure you can hold or touch it to get a sense of its energy.

A Word About Drums

Drums remain an extremely popular and almost omnipresent shamanic tool. The most common are single-headed drums with a relatively soft mallet head. Such a drum is constructed on a wooden frame with a single rawhide stretched across the frame. The length of the mallet is usually smaller than the diameter of the drum and the mallet-head is of cloth fur. Rawhide, by the way, is uncured leather, which is stretched across the frame over a long period of time.

When if comes to selecting your drum, it is best to do so in person, rather than order from a catalogue or a website. If at all possible visit the drum maker and play several drums.

In selecting your drum, play several. Use a soft, steady beat for a minute or two, and listen for the drums that call to you. Inspect both drum and mallet carefully. Notice particularly the cords that hold the drumhead and the places where these cords are attached to the head and

make sure that there is no thinning or splintering here.
Don't worry, however, if the frame is somewhat warped
In drumming for shamanic purposes, you will often drum
for extended periods, so pick a drum and mallet that are
comfortable to hold, and not too heavy or cumbersome.
The most comfortable drums tend to be medium size—
around 17 inches in diameter-- and have a pad or cushion
for the hand at the back.

The construction of the mallet, if you select a drum that
has one, is important too.. Inspect the mallet carefully to
see that the mallet head is attached firmly to the handle.
You can find drums with heads made of many types of
rawhide. Most common are elk, cow, horse, and deer. With
good care, the rawhide drumheads rarely split.

Commercial plastic headed drums, though not as
"authentic looking", have some advantages. For one thing,
they retain their tone in all weather, and unlike their wood
and leather counterparts, are not affected by humidity.
They also cost considerably less. Since they are made of
wood and plastic, they are also good for those who don't
want to own animal hides.

Working with Your Shaman Drum

When a drum is new, it needs to be awakened, and broken in. Play it particularly gently at first and, if you have the opportunity, take it around older drums and play along with them. This awakening process partly involves the joining and synching of the unique resonance patterns of the drumhead and the frame.

You will find a relationship developing with your drum as you use it and will quickly discover that your drum also has moods and fluctuations in energy. Be patient with your drum, and with yourself. You will get spiritual benefit and guidance from just playing your drum regularly, even if you aren't the greatest drummer in the world.

It is best to reserve particular drums and rattles for sacred work and to have other drums and rattles for drum circles, or social music making. It is important to honor and respect the drum by not displaying it ostentatiously, by keeping the drum "face up" when setting it down, and by smudging it periodically with sage.

Destroying Consecrated or Charged Items

Items can generally be un-charged with a simple ritual. It is advisable to cleanse it afterwards with water, fire, air and and/or earth. After this treatment the item is discharged and purified properly. How you actually handling this kind of elementary cleansing is totally up to you and your spirits, your own experiences and of your own preference. There are items that can only be discharged by their complete and total destruction like burning, melting or dissolving. All these actions must be done with the intention of de-consecrating or un-charging the item. With gifts from nature it is the best to give them back to nature with a small ritual.

The Shamanic Headdress

The headdress is a very useful and omni-present shamanic tool, and of course, is quite a show. One function of the headdress could be that it is showing to the person attending a rite exactly who is leading the rite. It can also empower the individual, or have some sort of sacred meaning. It can also be a part of the costume for the animal dances.

Feathers from birds symbolize the ability of the shaman to travel the spirit world with his soul. Long feathers (most of the time two of them) are symbolic horns or antennas. During the shamanic journey the shaman usually transforms his conception of himself into that of his power-animal. The shamanic costume and the headdress are enforcing this and showing this transformation to the material world.

The headdress can also be an instrument for inducing trance-states. By wearing the headdress only during rituals the shaman is actually programming himself to get in the correct state of mind for the trance. The jingling of bells or metal tassels on the headdress can drive away evil spirits, and induce trance by acoustic stimulation, as well.

The headdress serves the function of protecting the shaman during his journeys. The feathers of nocturnal hunting-birds protect him from night spirits, and eagle, or hawk feathers, for example, protect him from day spirits and animals. The protective powers are even active if the shaman is far away from the headdress. The headdress warns him of things happening nearby its position, functioning as a remote control of personal things.

A shamanic headdress can be very detailed in its various meanings and abilities. It is a good idea to ask your spirits for details in its construction and powers. If you make it yourself from scratch, it can take you a long time to complete your headdress. It is worth it.

A last and important note: a shamanic headdress is not really necessary in normal shamanic works. You may feel, however, that it is something that you, the spirits, and others can enjoy.

Smudging

Smudging is an age-old tribal tradition which has been used for centuries to bring harmony and peace to a space. It is the burning of herbs or incense for cleansing, purification, protection of physical and spiritual bodies, banishment of negative energies and consecration of sacred space. There are many options for smudging. You can use braided herbs and botanicals or loose herbs.

Shamanic smudging releases the energy and fragrance of the herbs and botanicals so they can heal, cleanse and purify. In many traditions shamanic smudging will consist of a ceremony where a prayer team sends smoke in the four directions in order to consecrate the entirety of the space. The smudging can serve different purposes: it can cleanse the space, turn an area into a holy space, or aid in the process of divination. Various prayers will program the smoke to do the specific action. Shamanic smudging can also be used in daily life and for practical concerns. It can protect from negative energy, or ground the room.

The following is a list of common or popular herbs used in smudging:

Pinon resin

This generally channels fire energy, but it can effectively be used in the four elements for general purposes. it serves to cleanse, strengthen, warm, and can also be used for its spiritual healing properties. It has a very pleasant and mild fragranc, and the thick smoke is invigorating.

Copal Gold resin

This is generally an urban power that conducts fire and water elements, but it can also be used for general purposes. Dissent is sweet, and earthy. It is generally used in divinatory and cleansing ceremonies. Some say that it was used by Middle American and native peoples prior to vision quests.

Myrrh resin

This is primarily an earth elements but it can also be used for general purposes in the four directions. It is very smoky and burns a low temperature, with an earthy scent. It has been used since ancient Egyptian times for rituals involving passing, consecration, and healing. It is excellent to use for a meditative space.

Frankincense resin

This primarily conducts fire energy but it also can be used for general purposes in the four directions. The smoke is a rich, and full. It is excellent to use for meditative purposes. It has been used since ancient Egyptian times for consecration, blessing, and ceremonies of birth and death

Desert Sage

This is generally an error element although it is excellent for general purposes of consecration and cleansing. It is earthy yet   light in scent. It is excellent when used to purify a space before prayer or a ceremony. It can also be used to smudge sacred items such as magical pools, talismans, or amulets. It is an excellent all-purpose herb to use for cleansing of the home, and the aura.

Juniper

This is a fire and water herb but can also be used with good results for general purposes. It has a sharp earthy scent, and is an excellent stimulant. It is excellent to use to consecrate spaces that will be used for divinatory purposes, and for work involving the stimulation of the communication chakra.

White broadleaf sage

This is an excellent herb for general purposes, and working with all four elements. It has a light, earthy scent. It is excellent for meditation, and divination, smudging, cleansing, and purification. It is an excellent all-purpose herb

Yerba

This is excellent to consecrate a space that will be used for meditation or divination. It is excellent for enhancing psychic abilities, and for giving spiritual strength. It has an invigorating, strong scent. It has a lot of feminine, moon energy.

Hibiscus

These herbs primarily contain elements of fire and water, and are not the best choice for working with all four elements in all four directions. It has a sharp, invigorating, sweet smell that lingers for hours after it is burned. It is excellent to use in ceremonies of divination and to stimulate psychic awareness. It is also good for stimulating the chakras, and encouraging proper energy flow through space

Rose flowers

Rose primarily as a water elements, and is best when used as such. Despite the sweet, mild smell of the blooming flower, it produces a heavy scent when burnt ,which lasts a long time. It is excellent for ceremonies is passing, and is also good for increasing psychic abilities. It is also useful for using a love spells, and spells whose aim is to stimulate sexual appetite.

Sweet Grass

This earthy smelling herb primarily contained air energy by can be used in ceremonies involving all four directions and all four elements. It produces a light fragrance, that isn't terribly long lasting, so it is good to burn for all-purpose spaces. It invites good spirits, and vanquishes the bad. It is excellent to combine with other burning herbs. It is the perfect scent to burn for spaces used for yoga or meditation, and is also good for cleansing space.

Can I Smudge Myself?

Smudging yourself can serve several purposes. It can cleanse your aura, stimulate the chakras, and ensure proper energy flow. Smudging also stimulate your psychic abilities, and is helpful when you are seeking to ground yourself. Some smudge themselves after they have been exposed to negative energy, or energy vampires. It is also appropriate to smudge yourself before arriving at a ceremony, or ritual. You can also smudge yourself when you are feeling ill, sad, depressed, stressed, or overly hyper. Smudging can be an excellent way to stimulate the senses and capture a mood.

How Do I Smudge Myself?

If you are using a stick or bundle of herbs, light the stick with the flame of consecrated candle. Hold the stick over the flame until it starts to smolder, and smoke. Using a feather, a fan, paper, or your hand, direct the smoke towards your body, starting at the top of your head and eventually directing towards your feet. If you are using a fire bowl or loose herbs, light the herbs until they start to smolder and smoke. After you are satisfied that the herbs will continue smoldering, set the bowl on the ground, and stand over it or close to it. Let the smoke drift upwards.

Some feel that smudging is most effective when you, or the subject, are unclothed, however, if you are uncomfortable, it will be difficult to relax. Ultimately, you should wear what ever makes you feel comfortable.

Smudging other people

You do not need to be a shaman in order to effectively clean someone's aura. The subject can sit, stand, or lie down. You may play music, or light candles, or do whatever you feel is appropriate to set the correct mood. When the subject seems sufficiently relaxed, light your stick or bundle of herb on the flame of a consecrated candle. When you are satisfied that it will stay lit, slowly move towards the subject, meditating on your purpose as you do so. Start with the top of his or her head. Hold the bundle of herbs so it is touching his or her or her auric field, gradually moving down the body until you have smudged each chakra, and continuing down to the feet. When you are finished, let the other person relax for as long as he or she wishes.

Part III: Holistic Medicine

A Holistic Approach to Medicine

The shaman takes a holistic approach to healing, and often uses herbs or plants, in addition to shamanic extractions and a host of other techniques, to heal those who come to her for help. Herbal medicine is often confused with holistic medicine. In reality, they are not necessarily one and the same, though they can be used together with excellent results.

Holism is an approach in which the entire body, and all of its systems, is considered when treating a malady. This system is opposed to just treating the symptoms of the malady and ignoring the rest of the body and mind.

A holistic approach to healing recognizes that the emotional, mental, spiritual and physical elements of each person comprise a system, and takes into consideration the cause of the illness as well as symptoms. Examples of such holistic therapies include Acupuncture, Ayurveda, Chinese medicine, Chiropractic, Osteopathic manipulation, Naturopathic medicine, Qi Gong, Reiki, and Reflexology.

As you can see, this is very much the approach of the Shaman, who not only attempts to treat the body, but also the spirit and the mind. Ailments of the body cannot always be corrected through reiki, meditation, shamanic practice, or other such methods. Sometimes it is necessary to correct the imbalance with the use of outside agents, such as plants and herbs.

Herbal Medicine

Neo-shamans, like many devotees to New Age practices, often use herbal medicine to treat a variety of physical ills. What follows are several lists: a list by ailment, and a list of herbs followed by what the herb can treat.

Native American Herbal Remedies by Affliction

Asthma

Skunk Cabbage: Skunk Cabbage was used by the Winnebago and Dakota tribes as an expectorant.

.

Backache

Arinca: The Catawba Indians used a tea of arnica roots for treating bruises, and back pains. It can also be applied topically, or used as a wash to treat sprains and bruises.

Gentian: Catawba Indians steeped the roots in hot water and applied the infusion topically, or used it as a wash.

Bronchitis

Creosote Bush: A tea of the leaves was used for bronchial and other respiratory problems.

Pleurisy Root: Many tribes drank a tea of the boiled roots as a remedy for pneumonia and used it as a general expectorant

Childbirth

Partridgeberry: The Cherokee used a tea of the leaves to encourage contractions and hasten child birth.

Blue Cohosh: To promote a rapid delivery, an infusion of the root in warm water was drunk as a tea as the delivery date became close.

Broom Snakeweed: Tribal women drank a tea of the whole plant to promote the expulsion of the placenta.

Black Western Chokecherry.: The Omaha peoples boiled the berries and applied the result as an external wash to stop bleeding after delivery.

White Willow Tree: Women were given a tea of the inner bark to relieve pain during childbirth

Colds

Boneset: Creeks used boneset to treat body aches, and the Mohegans to alleviate the fever accompanying an illness.

Peppermint : Peppermint tea was widely used as an expectorant and fever reducer.

Colic

Catnip: Various tribes made a tea of catnip leaves for infant colic.

Coughs

Wild Cherry: The Ojibwa prepared a tea of the bark of wild cherry trees to act as an expectorant.

Aloe Vera: Native peoples in the Southwest and in Mexico used the aloe vera juice to treat colds.

Diabetes

Wild Carrot: The Mohegans made a tea of the flowers when they were in full bloom to control blood sugar. Other tribes chewed the seeds and used them as contraceptives.

Diarrhea

Blackcherry: A deduction of blackberry roots was frequently used as a remedy for diarrhea among Indians of northern California.

Digestive Disorders

Dandelion: A tea of the roots was commonly taken for heartburn.

Spearmint: Spearmint was commonly used to improve digestion

Fevers

Dogwood.: The Delaware Indians steeped the bark and drank the liquid to bring down fevers.

White Willow Bark White willow was, and still is, a common cure for fever, headaches, chills, and pain.

Headache

Raspberry : Tea made of the leaves was a common cure for headaches.

Heart and Circulatory Problems

Green Hellebore: The Cherokee used the green hellebore to relive body pains.

Dogbane: The Potawatomis boiled the fruits and drank the resulting liquid to treat heart afflictions.

Hemorrhoids

White Oak: The Menominee tribe treated piles by squiring white oak tea into the rectum.

Inflammations and Swellings

Witch Hazel: The Menominees of Wisconsin boiled the leaves and used the tea as a wash to ease muscle aches and pains.

Arnica: Arnica was used by many tribes as a wash or poultice to treat bruises and muscle aches.

Insect Repellents and Insecticides

Goldenseal The root was made into a poultice by the Cherokee and used as insect repellent, and protection from poisonous plants. The tea of the plant was also used as a tonic.

Sedatives

Hops: The Mohegans prepared a tea of hops as a remedy for nervousness.

Thrush

Geranium: The Cherokee boiled geranium root to use as a mouthwash for children afflicted with thrush.

Native American Herbal Remedies by Herb

Ayahuasca

Ayahuasca is a medicine used by tribes indigenous to the Amazon. It is generally comprised of Banisteriopsis Caapi & Psychotria Viridis, two powerful psychedelic plants that can induce visions and hallucinations. It is recommended that this medicine is always used with the proper guidance of experienced shamans or healers, and it certainly should not be kept anywhere near children or unsupervised teenagers.

Cacao

Cacao, or raw chocolate, is rich in antioxidants, minerals, and vitamins, and ingesting it will trigger the release of dopamine and other chemicals typically released when we are in love, or engaging in sex. It can be used as an aphrodisiac, but it should be noted that best results come from using raw cacao beans instead of processed chocolate. Raw cocoa beans, though excellent, are markedly different in taste than the refined chocolate we are used to in North

America. It is, however, possible to order cacao beans raw and unprocessed.

Cat's Claw

Cat's Claw is used by Native peoples to stimulate the immune system. It can also be a tonic, an astringent, and bonds with free radicals, thereby protecting cells from damage.

Coca

The Coca plant, it should be noted, is illegal. The plant is the starting source for cocaine. The cultivation of cocaine by the peoples of South America has led to deforestation and a host of other ills, but before it was discovered that the plant could be ground up, combined with gasoline, and then burned to be made into cocaine, it was a medicinal plant in the Amazon. It is very high in nutrients, rich in both proteins and vitamins, and of course can act as a stimulant, vaso-constrictor, and anti-depressant. It was, and still is, chewed in its raw form by natives, as well as made into tea. The cocaine found on the street, however, has been stripped of its benefits because of the highly chemical means in which it is processed. Sadly, the misuse of this plant has robbed us of our ability to benefit from its benign properties.

Dragon's Blood

The Amazon people use the sap to heal cuts, stop bleeding, and encourage healing.

Maca Root

Maca root, when made into a deduction and drank as tea, is an excellent tonic, and helps balance the hormones. It has a stimulating effect, and has been called "Peruvian Ginseng" because it is so similar in effect to Ginseng. Maca is filled with proteins, vitamins, and minerals, and alkaloids. It has also been used in Peru as an aphrodisiac.

Peruvian Torch Cactus

This cactus is a powerful psychedelic. It should not be used without the supervision of an experienced shaman, if at all.

Agave

This sturdy, sharp succulent is now made into a popular liquor known as tequila. Before that, however, it was brewed into a drink called pulque, and used as medicine by the Mayans and Aztecs.

Damiana

This bush is very affective as an aphrodisiac for both men and women.

Salvia Divinorum

This powerful plant that is part of the sage family has recently experienced a renaissance amongst American youth culture. It is a powerful hallucinogen whose effects do not last nearly as long as other street hallucinogens, such as mushrooms or LSD. It also has the benefit of being legal, at least for the time being. It can, however, be dangerous if used unsupervised. Great care should be taken with this herb.

Morning Glory

Morning Glory is used by the Mayans for general healing purposes.

Sun Opener (Sinicuichi)

The Sun Opener is a shamanic medicine that alters consciousness and improves memory. Users have reported auditory hallucinations and yellow tinted visions.

Hawaiian Baby Woodrose Seeds

This plant is used by shamans for hallucinogenic purposes.

Kava Kava

Kava is generally consumed as an herbal tea to relieve stress and anxiety.

Herbal Medicine for the Urban Shaman

It is expensive, difficult, and occasionally impossible to get some of the herbs that have been traditionally used by Shamans and native peoples. Some are illegal; some are just not widely available. This does not, however, mean that practicing herbal medicine is impossible for those of us wishing to live the way of the Shaman while residing in an urban setting. Here is a list of household items that can be used for healing purposes, as well as herbal remedies made with ingredients found in most grocery stores.

Apple
Malus domestica

Apples are one of the most widely cultivated and consumed fruits. Research suggests that the consumption of apples may reduce the risk of colon cancer, prostate cancer and lung cancer. Apples also contain a naturally occurring antioxidant that has shown some promise in protecting cells from the effects of stress

Apple consumption can help remove food stuck between the teeth, but the acid contained in the fruit is also capable of eroding tooth enamel over time, so eating an apple should not be a substitute for tooth brushing. Raw, overripe, or baked apple can be made into a poultice to treat a sprain, or put over the eyes to relieve eyestrain. Apple water can also reduce a fever.

Apricot/Apricot Seed
Prunus armeniaca

The apricot fruit comes from a tree that is thought to have originated in China, and was brought to Europe by the Moors when they invaded and took over Spain.
Laetrile, which has long been considered a treatment for cancer, is extracted from apricot seeds. As early as the year 502, apricot seeds were used to treat tumors and ulcers. The American Medical Association, however, does not substantiate the effectiveness of laetrile.

Apricots have also been used as an aphrodisiac, and to stimulate uterine contractions.

Arrowroot
Maranta arundinacea (Marantaceae)

Arrowroot is native to South America and the Caribbean. The indigenous peoples in these areas have long used its root as a poultice for sores, and as an infusion to treat urinary tract infections. It can also be used as a soothing agent on inflamed mucous membrane tissue, a nutrient in convalescence, and for easing digestion. It helps to relieve acidity, indigestion and colic, and can act as a gentle laxative. It may be applied as an ointment, demulcent, or poultice mixed with some other antiseptic herbs such as comfrey.

Beet
Beta Vulgaris

Though the root is used for cooking in the west, it is possible to use the tops of the beet as salad greens. The root is extremely versatile, and can be peeled, steamed or baked, and then eaten warm with butter; or peeled, shredded raw, and then eaten as a salad. The Romans used beet root as a treatment for fevers and constipation, to bind wounds, and as an aphrodisiac.

Cabbage

Cabbages are flowering plants of the family Brassicaceae, and are related to the wild mustard plant. In European folk medicine, cabbage leaves are used to treat acute inflammation. One leaf can be dipped in water and placed on a wound in order to alleviate discomfort. It should be replaced after it gets warm from the wound. It also can help infected wounds and draw out pus in the same manner. One of the chemicals in cabbage can also treat respiratory papillomavirus.

Cayenne Pepper
Capsicum Solanaceae

Cayenne, consumed in powdered form, or as raw fruit, has been used as medicine for centuries. It is the most effective blood stimulant ever studied. In addition, it has endorphin-stimulating properties. It can treat stomachaches, cramping pains, and gas. If rubbed on the skin, it can act as an irritant, which, oddly enough, can be beneficial if rubbed on an area of the skin that has already been irritated. It can also be gargled as a wash to improve a sore throat. Some studies suggest that it can act as an appetite suppressant, and can help even out spikes in blood sugar.

Cayenne peppers are high in Vitamin C, Vitamin B, potassium, and iron.

Celery

Apium graveolens

Although celery is now very common in culinary pursuits, it has many fine healing properties. It's mainly used in the treatment of rheumatism, arthritis and gout. The seeds are also used as a urinary antiseptic. It is a very good cleansing herb, and a powerful diuretic, and can help in expelling waste and toxins. The seeds also have a reputation as a carminative with a mild tranquilizing effect. The stems are less significant medicinally, but are certainly useful in the kitchen.

Cinnamon

Cinnamomum verum syn. C. zeylanicum (Lauraceae)

Cinnamon is native to Sri Lanka, and grows best in tropical forest climates. Cinnamon has long been used in India and Egypt for medicinal purposes. To this day, it is, of course, a common spice in cooking, and is used in perfumery. The infusion or powder is excellent to help alleviate stomach pains and cramps. There is also some evidence that cinnamon can help smooth out spikes in blood sugar. Cinnamon is also useful as a household insecticide and to keep away ants—if sprinkled on a trail of ants, the ants will die, and will be less likely to return. Traditionally, the herb was taken for colds, flu and digestive problems.

Cumin
Nigella sativa

Cumin seeds have a bitter flavor and smell a bit like strawberries. It is a common household herb for cooking and flavoring liquor. Ibn Sina, known to westerners as Avicenna, refers to black cumin as a seed that stimulates the body's energy and helps recovery from fatigue and dispiritedness. He also describes it as having a positive effect on treating digestive disorders, gynecological diseases and respiratory ailments.

The seeds have been used in the Middle East and Southeast Asian countries to treat Asthma, Bronchitis, Rheumatism and related inflammatory diseases, to increase lactation, in nursing mothers, to promote digestion, and to fight parasitic infections. Its oil has been used to treat skin conditions such as eczema and boils.

Garlic

Allium sativum (Liliaceae)

Garlic is originally from central Asia but was used as flavoring and medication by the Egyptians, Greeks, and Romans. Garlic is still incredibly useful. It is one of the most effective antibiotic plants commonly available, acting on bacteria, viruses and alimentary parasites. The cloves can counter nose, throat and chest irritations, and can act as an expectorant. It will also act as a palliative for congested sinuses and can help clear blocked nasal passages to bring relief in cases of bad allergies or a cold. Garlic is also known to reduce cholesterol, increase circulation, lower blood pressure, and lower blood sugar levels. It can also help to expunge parasites, such as worms, from the body.

Honey

For at least 2700 years, honey has been used to treat a variety of ailments through topical application. Antibacterial properties of honey are the result of a hydrogen peroxide like behavior on a chemical level, and high acidity. Topical honey has been used successfully in a comprehensive treatment of diabetic ulcers and antioxidants in honey have been shown to reduce the damage done to the colon in colitis.

Furthermore, some studies suggest that honey may be effective in increasing the populations of good bacteria in the digestive tract, which may help strengthen the immune system, improve digestion, lower cholesterol, and prevent cancer of the colon.

Some studies suggest that the topical use of honey may reduce odors, swelling, and scarring when used to treat wounds; it may also prevent the dressing from sticking to a wound that is healing.

Lemon
Citrus Limon (Rutaceae)

The Arabs first introduced the lemon to Europe when they were in control of Spain. It is now widely cultivated in Italy, California and Australia. It is an important and versatile natural medicine. It is cheap, readily available, and can easily be used at home.

Lemons have a high vitamin C content that helps improve resistance to infection, and can reduce the duration of a cold or a flu. It is taken as a preventative for stomach infections, circulatory problems and arteriosclerosis. Lemon juice and oil are effective in killing germs. Lemon juice also decreases inflammation and improves digestion. Drinking a cup of lemon tea can help soothe a fever, and eating a lemon slice can help relieve sinus congestion.

Nutmeg

Myristica fragrans/argentea/otoba

The essential oil taken from steaming ground nutmeg is currently used often in cosmetics and perfumery. There is anecdotal evidence that nutmeg and nutmeg oil can treat problems of the nervous and digestive systems.

Externally, the oil can be topically applied to provide relief from rheumatic pain and can be applied to an infected or decayed tooth to quell the pain. Using a few drops of nutmeg oil on a sugar lump, a small piece of fruit, or in a teaspoon of honey or maple syrup can act as a cure for nausea, gastroenteritis, chronic diarrhea, and indigestion.

A massage oil to treat muscle pain and ache can be made by mixing 10 drops of nutmeg in 10 ml almond oil.

Oatmeal

"Oatmeal" is used to describe any crushed or rolled oats from a variety of species of plants. It is an excellent, gentle food to eat when convalescing or ill. It can also be made into a paste to ease itching, hives, or insect bites. Dissolving it in the bath will soothe sunburned skin.

Onion
Allium cepa

This popular household food is native to Central Asia, and evidence suggests that onions may be effective in treating the common cold, heart disease, and diabetes. They can act as anti-inflammatory, and have anticholesterol, anticancer, and antioxidant components. In homeopathy, onion is used for rhinorrhea and hay fever.

Onions are very rich in chromium, a mineral that helps cells respond to insulin, plus vitamin C, and numerous flavonoids.

The higher the intake of onion, the lower the level of glucose found during oral or intravenous glucose tolerance tests. This means that onions could possibly be helpful in controlling spikes in blood sugar.

The regular consumption of onions has, like garlic, been shown to lower high cholesterol levels and high blood pressure, and to be a very effective anti-inflammatory and expectorant. In addition, quercitin and other flavonoids found in onions work with vitamin C to help kill harmful bacteria.

Oregano
Oreganum vulgare

Oregano is high in antioxidant activity, and has demonstrated anti-microbial activity against food-borne pathogens. In the Philippines, oregano is not commonly used for cooking but is rather considered as a primarily medicinal plant, useful for relieving children's coughs.

Thyme
Thymus L

There are about 350 plants that fit into the genus "thymus". It was widely used for embalming in ancient Egypt, and was used by the ancient Greeks to freshen and purify rooms. Currently, it is primarily known as a useful culinary herb, though it does have some medicinal properties.

The essential oil of common thyme is an antiseptic, and is anti-fungal agent. A tea made by infusing the herb in water can be used for to treat coughs, irritations of the respiratory tract, and bronchitis. Because it is antiseptic, thyme boiled in water and cooled can be gargled to soothe a sore throat. Thyme tea can cause uterine contractions, and as such, should not be taken by pregnant women.

White Vinegar

Vinegar can be used as a herbicide if diluted to 20% vinegar and 80% water. It may kill some top growth if a plant is particularly delicate, but will not kill the roots. Vinegar along with hydrogen peroxide is used in the livestock industry to kill bacteria and viruses before refrigeration storage.

Hippocrates prescribed vinegar for many ailments, from skin rash to ear infection. Multiple trials indicate that taking vinegar with food increases satiety dramatically, and even a single application of vinegar can lead to reduced food intake for a whole day. Small amounts of vinegar—i.e. two tablespoons per serving--added to food, or taken along with a meal, have been shown by to reduce the glycemic index of carbohydrate food for people with and without diabetes.

Useful Herbal Teas for the Shaman

Rosemary Tea

Useful for: general aches and pains, lack of energy

Directions: boil water, and add one teaspoon of crushed or dried rosemary. Pour through a strainer and serve. Honey may be used as a sweetener

Ginger Tea

Useful for: asthma, respiratory problems

Directions: add ¼ teaspoon of ginger to ½ cup of hot water. Take two tablespoons before bedtime.

Holy Basil Tea

Useful for: chronic bronchitis; chronic irritation of the upper respiratory tract

Directions: Add 1 tablespoon of basil to 2 cups of hot water. Take two tablespoons four times per day

Cinnamon Tea

Useful for: congestion; common cold

Directions: Add 3 g. bark to 1 ½ cups of hot water. Steep and drink at bedtime as tea.

Cayenne Pepper Shot

Useful for: extreme congestion, sinus infection

Directions: Mix 1 c. hot water, 1 tsp lemon juice, 1 garlic clove put through a garlic press, and 1 pinch cayenne pepper. Mix well and drink quickly.

Fennel Linseed Tea

Useful for: constipation

Directions: Mix 1/3 tea spoon Fennel seeds, powdered, 1/3 tea spoon Linseed seeds, powdered, 1/3 tea spoon Liquorice root, powdered, and 1 3/4 cups Water. Boil, covered, for 10 minutes. Filter the tea before drinking. Drink one cup, three times a day.

Black Pepper Tea

Useful for: diarrhea

Directions: Boil 5 crushed pepper seeds in 1 c. the water for 15 minutes in a covered container. Remove from the heat and strain. Take 1/2 tea spoon, twice a day.

Ginger Mint Tea

Useful for: fever

Directions: Mix 2g crushed ginger and 2g crushed mint leaves in 1 1/2 c. water and bring to a boil. Cover and cook for 15 minutes. Strain the deduction and drink.

Lemon Tea

Useful for: cold, fever

Directions: Bring 1c. of water to a boil. Pour a cup and add one lemon slice. Sip slowly.

Yarrow Tea

Useful for: piles

Directions: prepare the infusion by combining 1-2 tea spoon Herb/blossoms, crushed with 1c. water in a covered container. Let the mixture stand for 5-6 hours. Strain before drinking.

Coriander Infusion

Useful for: impotence

To make the infusion, cover 1 teaspoon chopped leaves with1 cup boiling water, close the lid of the teapot and leave for 15 minutes, then strain. Drink 2-4 tablespoons a day.

Remember: coriander leaf extract acts as an aphrodisiac, while Coriander seed extract suppresses the sex drive.

Mint Tea

Useful for: stomach pain

Directions: Combine 1 teaspoon crushed spearmint leaves with two cups water and raise the mixture to a boil in a covered container. Remove from the heat and let the tea stand for 15 minutes. Strain before drinking. Drink 1-2 cups a day.

Ginger Infusion

Useful for: painful menstruation

Mix 6 g Embelia, whole plant, powdered, 6 g Ginger, dried, powdered, and 1 3⁄4 cups Water and boil. Remove from the heat, strain and sweeten with 6 g of sugar. Drink 3⁄4 cup a day.

Onion Cold Relief

Useful for: extreme congestion; chest colds

Merely one sliced onion by the bed of a person who is suffering from horrific chest congestion.

Natural Flu Relief

Useful for: relief from the flu

Directions: Combine 2 teaspoons cayenne pepper, 1 1⁄2 teaspoons salt, 1 cup hot chamomile tea, 1 cup apple cider vinegar, and the juice from 1 lemon slice. Boil in a covered container. Strain before drinking.

Part IV: Neo- Shamanism and Other New Age Practices

Shamanism In Combination With Other New Age Practices

The New Age movement imported some ideas from shamanism as well as Eastern religions. It has an infinite of manifestations, but it often blends ideas from the East with concepts taken from Native American animism.

At the same time, there is an endeavor in occult and esoteric circles to re-invent shamanism in a modern form drawing from core shamanism, by the aforementioned Michael Harner. This conception of core-shamanism often involves ritual drumming and dance, elements taken from Native American rituals, and chaos magic. Some authors argue that yoga, meditation, and other Eastern practices have their roots in Shamanism, or vice-versa, and readily incorporate these practices into their work.

Sometimes people from Western cultures, with not a drop of Native blood and little background in the study of Native religions, claim to be shamans. This is considered offensive by many indigenous medicine men, who view these new age, western "shamans" as hucksters out for money or affirmation of self. Many native cultures fear they will be overwhelmed by, and eventually drowned out by self-styled "shamans".

Wicca, Magick, and Shamanism

Because shamanism is often lumped in with other New Age practices, and Shamanic tools are frequently sold alongside Wiccan tools, many wonder what they have in common, and how they are different. The current terminology generally differentiates the modern shaman and the hermetic magician or wiccan as follows: the shaman uses his abilities to make his knowledge of the invisible reality accessible to his society, while the Wiccan aims to find her own divine nature, to develop it, to realize it and to live it. Wiccans generally focus on harnessing and manipulating energy, while practitioners of neo-Shamanism merely seek to be empowered by it and connect with it.

Chakra Work and Shamanism

As of late, several books have been made available that merges neo-Shamanistic healing with Chakra work. A Chakra is a Sanskrit term that means "wheel". Chakras function and relate within the systemic suite of the human body/mind continuum, and the concept of the chakra grew alongside the mystical practice of yoga in Ancient India where it was first codified.

In this means of conceptualizing the body-mind continuum, there are seven main chakra points, each corresponding to a specific area of the body and to a specific color frequency. They are often depicted in charts as swirling tunnels of color that pass all the way through the spirit body and are surrounded by flowing energy. Those who can see auras say that in healthy people, the chakras appear as clear, bright colors, and in those suffering from spiritual or physical distress, they appear as darker, dull, or splotchy colors.

The chakras are connected to each other and to the many other tunnels in the human spirit body along the spine. These tunnels or energy, or channels of energy, should appear vertically aligned along the spine. Sometimes these interconnecting channels will get blocked, preventing the proper flow of energy throughout the body. The blockage can be the result of a physical or mental illness, or it can be a response to stress.

The first chakra is located at the sacrum, or the tailbone. The color associated with it is red. It deals with, and processes, instincts, survival, past lives, fears, and grounding.

The second chakra just below the belly button. Its color is orange. It deals with instinct, reflexes, sexual energy, reproduction, and creativity. □

The third chakra is located at the solar plexus, just above the belly button. Its color is yellow. It deals with action, leadership, aggression, and exertion, both physical and mental.

The fourth chakra is located at the chest, specifically the heart. Its color associated with it is green. It deals with emotions, self-esteem, and intimacy. □

The fifth chakra is located at the throat, but it also governs hearing and the ears as well. The color associated with it is blue. It deals with communication, channeling, telepathy, psychic abilities, and self-expression. □

The sixth chakra is located at the brow and eyes, and is also known as the third eye. Its color is indigo. It deals with perception, and point of view.

The seventh chakra is located at the crown or the top of the head. Its color is violet. It deals with spiritual wisdom, and is the entrance and the exit between the body and the spirit world.

It is possible to feel these energy vortexes and what purposes they serve. To do so, pick a time when you can enjoy relative silence, and a location where you won't be disturbed. Lie down with your hands at your sides, your heels touching, your feet open, and your body relaxed.

Take note of how you feel, and if you note any emotional or physical disturbances located at the point of the chakra. If you notice any blockages in energy, this may be a good time to burn incense, or smudge yourself in order to clear the pathways. If you are unable to release these blockages yourself, consult an experienced healer for advice.

Remember to monitor your chakras, and periodically perform a check of your chakric system.

Shamanism and Reiki

Reiki is a technique for balancing energy and healing, and it is not uncommon to hear of healers who claim to be versed both in the art of shamanism and reiki. Whether you feel that it is appropriate to use the reiki system in your work is up to you.

This Japanese form of energy work was developed Mikao Usui in the early 20th century. He claimed he received the ability to heal others after three weeks of fasting and meditation.

During a reiki session, practitioners use a technique similar to the laying on of hands, which they say will channel "healing energy" from their bodies into the bodies of the subject. They do this without depleting their own energies. Practitioners state that energy flows through their palms and that they can treat themselves, as well as others. The philosophy of reiki is that there is a very basic 'life force' in all, which can be accessed by practitioners. Anyone can gain access to the ability to tap into, and manipulate this energy if he or she works with a Reiki Master. In order to learn reiki, one's chakras must first be aligned, and he or she must be taught to recognize the vibrations of the life force of another.

The premise of reiki is that the energy will flow through the practitioner's hands whenever the hands are placed on, or held near a potential recipient. The recipient can be naked, or clothed. Some place great significance on the intention and focus of the practitioner, while others claim that the recipient is drawing the energy from the practitioner and the intentions of the practitioner are not so relevant. Those who believe the latter also share the belief is that the 'energy' is 'intelligent', making diagnosis, and focus, unnecessary. Others believe that if the recipient does not wish to be healed, or has a bad attitude, that his or her ability to heal will be compromised.

Some say that the energy involved in a Reiki treatment is said to be 'from the Universe,' rather than the personal energy of the practitioner. Others say that the energy enters the practitioner through the crown chakra at the top of the head, before being emitted from the hands. Because the practitioner is channeling the energy of the universe, and not using his own energy, he is able to heal himself. Reiki is not only used to address illnesses of the body and spirit, it is used as preventative medicine, as it is said that the energy encourages healing before any noticeable symptoms have emerged.

Reiki is described by devotees as a holistic therapy which brings about healing on physical, mental, emotional and spiritual levels. It is said that healing may occur in any or all of these domains in a single treatment.

A typical whole-body Reiki treatment can be merged with other forms of treatment, such a shamanic extraction, or smudging, making it easy for the Shaman to incorporate Reiki into his healing activities. In such a treatment, the practitioner asks the recipient to lie down and relax.

The treatment proceeds with the practitioner placing his hands on the recipient in various positions, or, the practitioner may choose to place her hands on the auric field instead. The hands are usually kept still for 3 to 5 minutes before moving to the next position. Overall, the hand positions usually give a general coverage of the head, the front and back of the torso, the knees and feet. This process lasts anywhere from a half hour to an hour and a half.

Some practitioners use a fixed set of hand positions. Others use their intuition to guide them as to where treatment is needed, scanning as they go to note any injuries or energy vacuums.

It is reported that the recipient often feels warmth or tingling in the area being treated, even when a non-touching approach is being used. Most also say they feel incredible relaxes as the treatment progresses. Although it is possible to heal a client or patient within the first session, usually it takes a series of three or more treatments, typically at intervals of 1 to 7 days.

It is also possible to do a localized treatment, in which only one particular part of the body is treated.

Believers of reiki don't feel that humans have the monopoly on life force. This point of view fits nicely with shamanism, which is another reason why reiki may be a good addition to the shamanic quiver. Animals and plants can be treated with reiki. They are usually treated for shorter periods than humans. The duration of treatment, and number of hand positions used, depends on factors such as the size of the recipient and the severity of the condition being addressed.

It is possible to use reiki to not only prevent physical injuries that have yet to manifest symptoms, but to keep the auric field strong and the chakras in line. The cornerstone of Reiki spiritual practice is a daily one hour self-treatment, conducted in a meditative state. This practice is understood to induce spiritual growth and the possibilities of tapping into the vibrations of the universe.

How Does One Get Certified in Reiki?

The first degree Reiki course teaches the basic theories and procedures of how to work with Reiki energy. The channel through which Reiki energy passes to the practitioner is said to be opened or widened through four "attunements" in which the chakras are aligned and the auric field is assessed. Students learn hand placement positions on the recipient's body, and the basic principles of energy work. The course is usually about two days, and after its completion, it is possible to treat others.

In the second degree Reiki course, the student is introduced to three symbols which are said to magnify and strengthen the healing effect and allow for distance healing. Another attunement is given which is said to further increase the capacity to channel the energy of the universe, as well as empowering the use of the symbols. One must have taken a first degree course before signing up for the second, and after completion of a second course, the student can perform reiki over long distances.

After completion of the third phase of training, the student becomes a Reiki Master. One or more attunements are carried out and the student learns a further symbol, and how to channel its energy. Having completed the master training, the new Reiki Master can attune other people to Reiki, teach reiki, complete distance reiki, and even heal through time as well as space. The first and second degrees are prerequisites for the master training. In the case of comprehensive training, the third level is often broken into two or three smaller stages of attunements and teaching, as it is a longer course of study than the first two phases.

Many independent teachers combine Reiki with other techniques, such as working with crystals, color therapy, spirit guides or visualization. With the many varied ways that have been used to teach Reiki, there have emerged points of controversy between different groups, teachers and practitioners. Controversies exist on topics such as the nature of the Reiki energy itself, fees charged for courses and treatments, training methods, secrecy of symbols and attunement methods. Each center for reiki will have its own approach to training its students.

NeoShamanism versus Technoshamanism

Nechnoshamanism is a term used to describe a movement that seeks to integrate modern technology into neo-shamanistic practices. Members of this movement are generally affiliated with the rave community, and believe in using ethnogenic drugs, as well as street drugs and psychotherapy as a path to enlightenment.

Technoshamans generally embrace the view that mystical experiences are at least partially biological in nature and feel that it is then perfectly okay to induce a trance state, or mystical state, through drugs, music, or other technology-based means.

The Technoshamanists Toolbox

The toolbox of the technoshaman differs a bit from the toolbox of the neo shaman. Technoshamanists will turn to sensory deprivation chambers, transcranial magnetic stimulation devices, neurofeedback machines, music, and synthetic drugs, by themselves, or in groups. They use these tools as paths to shamanic journeys.

MDMA, magic mushrooms, LSD, and other psychoactive drugs are generally embraced by technoshamanists, who use them alone or in social settings to achieve a loss of the ego, further spiritual development, or realize a spiritual goal. Some say the drugs themselves are mystical substances—even synthesized drugs like LSD and MDMA-- while others say that psychoactive drugs are simply tools and that the altered states of consciousness that they produce may or may not be constructive, depending on the setting in which the drugs are taken, and the intentions of the user.

It is no coincidence that techoshamans are generally affiliated with the rave community. They feel that repetitive beats and certain noises, like those used in techno music, can influence functions of the brain besides those related to hearing. These types of sounds are also called binaural beats, and the brainwaves that they trigger is a phenomenon called frequency following response. They use these sounds as a background for socializing, to dance to, or to merely relax while engaging in meditation.

Though there are still people who identify themselves as technoshamanists, the movement seems to have had its heyday in the 1990s.

Part V: American Indian Reaction to Neo-Shamanism

The American Indian Movement's Perspective on Neo-Shamanism

Indian culture is not a monolith, and there is no one Indian point of view, or position, on neo-shamanism. Some seem to at least credit neo-shamanists with valuing Native contributions to world religion and philosophy; others see neo-shamanism as just another stereotype of Indians pushed on them by colonists. Still others are outraged that so-called shamans that have no Indian blood are appropriating their traditions.

The following, taken from the American Indian Movement Website, summarizes the last of these points of view:

Declaration of War Against Exploiters of Lakota Spirituality

At the Lakota Summit V, an international gathering of US and Canadian Lakota, Dakota and Nakota Nations, about 500 representatives from 40 different tribes and bands of the Lakota unanimously passed a "Declaration of War Against Exploiters of Lakota Spirituality." The following declaration was unanimously passed on June 10, 1993

Declaration of War

WHEREAS we are the conveners of an ongoing series of comprehensive forums on the abuse and exploitation of Lakota spirituality; and

WHEREAS we represent the recognized traditional spiritual leaders, traditional elders, and grassroots advocates of the Lakota people; and

WHEREAS for too long we have suffered the unspeakable indignity of having our most precious Lakota ceremonies and spiritual practices desecrated, mocked and abused by non-Indian "wannabes," hucksters, cultists, commercial profiteers and self-styled "New Age shamans" and their followers; and

WHEREAS with horror and outrage we see this disgraceful expropriation of our sacred Lakota traditions has reached epidemic proportions in urban areas throughout the country; and

WHEREAS our precious Sacred Pipe is being desecrated through the sale of pipestone pipes at flea markets, powwows, and "New Age" retail stores; and

WHEREAS pseudo-religious corporations have been formed to charge people money for admission into phony "sweatlodges" and "vision quest" programs; and

WHEREAS sacrilegious "sundances" for non-Indians are being conducted by charlatans and cult leaders who promote abominable and obscene imitations of our sacred Lakota sundance rites; and

WHEREAS non-Indians have organized themselves into imitation "tribes," assigning themselves make-believe "Indian names" to facilitate their wholesale expropriation and commercialization of our Lakota traditions; and

WHEREAS academic disciplines have sprung up at colleges and universities institutionalizing the sacrilegious imitation of our spiritual practices by students and instructors under the guise of educational programs in "shaminism;" and

WHEREAS non-Indian charlatans and "wannabes" are selling books that promote the systematic colonization of our Lakota spirituality; and

WHEREAS the television and film industry continues to saturate the entertainment media with vulgar, sensationalist and grossly distorted representations of Lakota spirituality and culture which reinforce the public's negative stereotyping of Indian people and which gravely impair the self-esteem of our children; and

WHEREAS individuals and groups involved in "the New Age Movement," in "the men's movement," in "neo-paganism" cults and in "shamanism" workshops all have exploited the spiritual traditions of our Lakota people by imitating our ceremonial ways and by mixing such imitation rituals with non-Indian occult practices in an offensive and harmful pseudo-religious hodgepodge; and

WHEREAS the absurd public posturing of this scandalous assortment of psuedo-Indian charlatans, "wannabes," commercial profiteers, cultists and "New Age shamans" comprises a momentous obstacle in the struggle of traditional Lakota people for an adequate public appraisal of the legitimate political, legal and spiritual needs of real Lakota people; and

WHEREAS this exponential exploitation of our Lakota spiritual traditions requires that we take immediate action to defend our most precious Lakota spirituality from further contamination, desecration and abuse;

THEREFORE WE RESOLVE AS FOLLOWS:

1. We hereby and henceforth declare war against all persons who persist in exploiting, abusing and misrepresenting the sacred traditions and spiritual practices of our Lakota, Dakota and Nakota people.

...

5. We assert a posture of zero-tolerance for any "white man's shaman" who rises from within our own communities to "authorize" the expropriation of our ceremonial ways by non-Indians...

Wilmer Stampede Mesteth; (Oglala Lakota); Traditional Spiritual Leader & Lakota Culture Instructor; Oglala Lakota College, Pine Ridge, South Dakota
Darrell Standing Elk; (Sicangu Lakota); President, Center for the SPIRIT, San Fancisco, California, & Pine Ridge, South Dakota
Phyllis Swift Hawk; (Kul Wicasa Lakota); Tiospaye Wounspe Waokiye; Wanblee, South Dakota

Other Native American Perceptions of Neo-Shamanism

Other, less militant voices feel the same way but describe it in gentler tones, lamenting that their cultures, traditions, and beliefs are being offered for sale by non-Natives. This sale functions in many ways to reduce Native Americans to stereotypes, foster misunderstanding of their rituals, and conflates them with Siberians. Some express irritation that non-Indians have shaped the public perception of Indians more than actual Indians, and lament that their religious practices have been reduced to forms of entertainment.

In any case, when striving to walk in the way of the shaman, it is always important to be culturally sensitive, and to respect the religions from which neo-shamanism is derived. It may be possible to visit a reservation and observe, or even participate in, a ceremony or ritual. Be very wary, however, of anyone charging to host a sweat lodge or ceremony. American Indians stress vehemently that these things should not be for sale.

INDEX

LaVergne, TN USA
25 August 2010
194614LV00002B/43/P